THE SHORT AND BLOODY HISTORY OF PIRATES

THE SHORT AND BLOODY HISTORY OF PIRATES

John Farman

Lerner Publications Company/Minneapolis

First American edition published in 2002 by Lerner Publications Company

Copyright © 2000 by John Farman

All U.S. rights reserved. No part of this book may be reproduced, stored in a retrieval system, or transmitted in any form or by any means—electronic, mechanical, photocopying, recording, or otherwise—without the prior written permission of Lerner Publications Company, except for the inclusion of brief quotations in an acknowledged review.

This book is available in two editions:
Library binding by Lerner Publications Company, a division of Lerner Publishing Group
Soft cover by First Avenue Editions, an imprint of Lerner Publishing Group
241 First Avenue North
Minneapolis, MN 55401 U.S.A.

Website address: www.lernerbooks.com

Library of Congress Cataloging-in-Publication Data

Farman, John.
    The short and bloody history of pirates / by John Farman.—1st
American ed.
        p.   cm.
    Includes index.
    Summary: A humorous presentation of the history and life of
pirates from the mid-seventeenth to mid-eighteenth centuries.
    ISBN: 0-8225-0843-5 (lib. bdg. : alk. paper)
    ISBN: 0-8225-0844-3 (pbk. : alk. paper)
    I. Pirates—Juvenile literature. [1. Pirates.] I. Title.
G535 F27 2002
364.16'4—dc 2001   2001050730

Manufactured in the United States of America
1 2 3 4 5 6—JR—07 06 05 04 03 02

CONTENTS

WHO AND WHAT AND
WHERE WERE PIRATES?

Does that seem a silly question? Almost everyone knows what pirates were—nasty, rough types with big hats, parrots, and wooden legs. They sailed in cool ships with lots of masts and cannons, yelling uncouth oaths and plundering and killing everyone who got in their way. Sure enough, all that stuff's more or less true, but it's really only half the story.

Almost as long as there've been boats, there've been pirates— Greek ones, Chinese ones, Viking ones, and Roman ones. Believe it or not, there are still a lot of mean modern pirates around today.

In fact, wherever there's a long and lonely trade route and an undefended prey, you'll find people trying to rob it. But the pirates I'm going to concentrate on—the ones you see in all the movies—are those from the mid-seventeenth to the mid-eighteenth centuries, the Golden Age of Piracy.

Before we start, I must tell you that there were several different types of pirates at the time. They went under different names, so I'd better explain, otherwise it might be confusing.

Privateers

Privateers were just as bad as other pirates, but they had a piece of paper called a commission (or license) from Britain's Admiralty Court. The commission more or less said that it was all right to do whatever they liked to an enemy ship (rob, murder, etc.) at times of war. The British government thought it had a good idea, because it was supposed to take the lion's

share of the booty. But many privateers—like the mighty Captain Henry Morgan—used their pirate's license freely, often attacking anything that moved, enemy or otherwise, and stashing most of their plunder before they got home. Many of the Caribbean islands gave out their own licenses to any old pirate who came along, purely for a share of the loot. The most famous

British privateers were the slave king Sir John Hawkins and, much earlier in the 1500s, Sir Francis Drake.

Corsairs

Corsair was the Italian name for privateer, but it later became the collective name for the infamous Barbary pirates who hailed from the coastal regions of North Africa—places like Algiers, Algeria; Tunis, Tunisia; and Tripoli, Libya. These scary seafarers, most of whom were Muslims (followers of Islam), terrorized the Mediterranean Sea in oar-powered warships.

Buccaneers

Buccaneers were British, French, or Dutch pirates, who hunted in and out of the Caribbean islands and later tried to get commissions to save their grimy necks when eventually brought to trial. Although ruthless and mean, they hardly ever attacked shipping from their own country. They got their name, by the way, from the first buccaneers who were hunters in the woods and valleys of Hispaniola (now Haiti and the Dominican Republic). These first buccaneers lived by cutting up pigs and cows into strips and smoking them. (Not like cigarettes, silly, but by hanging them up over a fire in a smokehouse—an ancient method of preserving meat.) The French word for this process was *boucaner,* and the boucaniers who did it were known for their disgusting smell and bedraggled, blood-stained appearance. Anyway, in the 1620s, all these boucaniers became fed up with

the smoked meat business and decided to move to the seaside, where they built a bunch of boats and formed a huge gang called the "Brethren of the Coast"—in other words buccaneers or pirates.

How Many?

Records seem to show that around 1720, right in the middle of the period I'm covering, there were between 1,800 and 2,400 American and British pirates prowling the seas, and roughly 13,000 naval seamen sworn to catch them. There are few records to tell us about all the others, but it's more than fair to say that traveling by sea carried enormous risk to life and limb in those not-really-so-far-off days.

Most pirates were recruited from captured merchant ships. Usually after all the fuss surrounding the plunder and pillage had died down, the pirate's quartermaster would step forward and ask if there were any merchant seamen who wanted to serve under the black flag (the skull and crossbones, or Jolly Roger, of which there were many versions).

JACK RACKHAM

THOMAS TEW

BLACKBEARD

BARTHOLEMEW ROBERTS

EDWARD ENGLAND

STEDE BONNET

Quite a few usually said yes, especially seeing what a good life the pirates seemed to be having compared to the drudgery they suffered (for almost no money). They threw caution to the wind and joined them. Most pirates, by the way, were aged between seventeen and fifty, with the majority being in their mid-twenties to early thirties.

Not All Laughs

But being a pirate wasn't all plain sailing, and it had more than its fair share of downsides. So be prepared for some hair-raising stories of dastardly piratical deeds guaranteed to make your blood run cold. So, heave-ho, me hearties, let's splice the main brace (whatever that means) and cast off.

ALL IN A DAY'S WORK

You may think that when pirates weren't robbing and murdering, they simply lazed around the decks, swigging rum, yo-ho-ho-ing, and generally having a great time. Well, you'd be right in some ways. Pirates had far less to do than merchant seamen, mostly because they usually had more than ten times the manpower.

Having said that, running a three-masted pirate boat of 300 tons or more, with enough rope to tie up, well, . . . lots of things, was no easy job, even if there were up to 200 of you. Old ships needed a lot of work to keep them sort of . . . shipshape.

Having said all that, pirates never really looked for hard work and preferred to indulge in their unpopular habit of stealing someone else's ship when theirs became a little, how shall we say, old and tired. Even so, a new ship would still have to be maintained if it was to compete on the high seas.

A ship, even in years gone by, was quite a complicated thing to manage. These days everything's made of metal, fiberglass, or plastic, so boats are relatively (and that's a huge relatively) maintenance free. But the old ships that sailed before people realized that metal could float were a complex web of wood, canvas, rope, and brass that required more than their fair share of looking after. Anyone who has had anything to do with wooden boats knows that you can't just build 'em, put 'em in the water, and sail 'em off into the sunset. No way.

Careening

Those old tubs needed tons of elbow grease. Sailors not only had to keep them upright, but they also had to keep the hull (the part of the boat in the water) as smooth as possible, so that they could sail at least as fast as the boats they were trying to catch or the ones that were trying to catch them. This laborious process of cleaning and maintaining the hull was called careening, and the pirates hated it. What with all the barnacles and seaweed that clung to their bottoms (the boats' not the pirates') or the dreaded teredo worms, which chomped their way into the wooden planking, rendering it about as seaworthy as a sieve, the massive vessels would have to be dragged aground every couple of months.

The whole crew would then be expected to scrub, scrape, replace any rotten timbers, fill up the leaky gaps between the planks with oakum (rope smothered in tar), and then paint the whole thing with a mixture of tallow, oil, and brimstone before giving it a thick coat of wax or tar.

This was a filthy but necessary job that had to be carried out on remote beaches (pirates couldn't pull into ports like anyone else) and often in tropical weather hot enough to bake a turtle or rainy enough to drown one.

And Then . . .

See, I told you being a pirate wasn't all laughs. As if that wasn't enough, while they were ashore, the pirate crew would then be expected to gather wood and search for streams or springs to fill all the water barrels to the brim. Then they would be sent out with guns and clubs to hunt whatever walked, crawled, slithered, or flew out in front of them. Often this would be easy,

as most of the islands that they stopped on were so remote that the pirates' prey had never seen humans before. They'd let the pirates walk right up to them without batting an eye— and that usually went for the natives as well! Well, some of the natives. The smart ones knew what the boys were up to and chased them off their islands with bows and arrows and poisoned darts from blowpipes. Sometimes the pirates they caught ended up as a somewhat salty stew for the whole village.

Carpenter Ahoy!

Above decks, work had to be done to mend any of the structure that might've been damaged in the last few months at sea. Whenever pirates attacked another ship, especially if it was a naval vessel, one of the first things they looked for were craftsmen. Most valuable of all would be a ship's carpenter, usually an ex-shipwright, who would come into his own after a battle, patching up holes in the hull, mending broken spars,

and fashioning wooden legs as replacements for the injured real ones. (Sometimes the carpenter would have had to cut off the real limbs as well!)

Surgeon Ahoy!

Another great prize would be a surgeon. Britain's Royal Navy always had a surgeon aboard, and pirates were so jealous that they'd try and capture him if they got a chance. Pirates, you see, were always suffering terrible injuries, either in fights among themselves, or when attacking other ships, or just from all the terrible things that can happen when you get a bunch of men on a relatively small boat—like tripping over the ship's cat.

Cooper Ahoy!

Everything that was to be consumed on a pirate boat, be it bully beef, hardtack, water, beer or stronger liquor, was kept in barrels. Therefore, the next most important person on board was the cooper or barrel maker. He would not only make new barrels but repair the old ones and be an expert in how things should be preserved.

Very often craftsmen on naval or merchant ships weren't too worried about being captured. For a start, the pay was much better among the pirates. A carpenter on a normal ship, for instance, although being one of the highest paid members of the crew, would make less than two dollars a week, and the cooper would earn half that. The surgeon would also be among the higher paid and would generally be regarded by the captain as an equal. A cook, by the way, only received seventy-five cents a week on a nonpirate ship (and this was mostly reflected in the quality of food he prepared). Secondly, if ever a pirate ship was captured and the crew were sent to trial, these craftsmen usually got off without penalty because they'd been forced to join the boat. Obviously, they didn't talk too much about the share of the loot they'd no doubt received.

Slaves Ahoy!

Talking of natives (which we weren't), pirates soon grasped the idea that they could be captured and made to do most of the hard work aboard ship. This became so popular that the buccaneers even hunted down the slave ships that plied the seas between Africa and the British colonies in the West Indies and stole their cargoes. This happened so often that in 1724 a group of very annoyed merchants trading with Jamaica wrote to the Council of Trade and Plantations in London, England, complaining bitterly that the pirates were causing the "havoc and destruction of the ships employed in the negro trade on which the being of our Colonies chiefly depends."

Stealing People for Profit

The whole slave trade started when European explorers, particularly the power-crazy Portuguese, while trekking through Africa realized that there were thousands of natives standing around who didn't seem to be doing anything. The Portuguese had always been short of people to work their land, so these unscrupulous men rounded up the natives and sent them back home to Portugal or Brazil. By the sixteenth century, everyone, including America, was in on the act. Everyone except Britain, which cried, "Why can't we have a share of all this lucrative trade?" (Actually, British privateers had been supplying the American colonies for years, but that was unofficial.)

The British generally got what they wanted in those days (how things have changed), and by 1713 all the Spanish colonies were getting their slaves from the British South Sea Company, which made vast profits out of the Africans' misery. By the end of the seventeenth century, the main customers for slaves were the British owners of southern American plantations. The poor, innocent Africans were treated worse than dogs—branded, chained, beaten, and raped at every opportunity.

Bargain Slaves

To give you some idea of the value of slaves (if you'd wanted to buy one), it was reported that, in the early seventeenth century, a fairly average slave could change hands for as little as the value of a humble onion. Keep in mind that, for all I know, onions could have been very expensive, but you know what I'm saying.

Pirates' Slaves

One good thing came out of the democratic way that pirate ships were run. Some of the stronger and braver slaves were promoted and began to share in the profits. But it must also be said that generally pirates were as bad as anyone else when it came to ill-treating their black brothers. Often slaves who were on the run from the disgusting conditions of the West Indies plantations would beg to come aboard. But they would often be treated even worse by their new pirate bosses.

The End of Slavery

This disgusting trade in human misery ended first in Denmark in 1792. Britain followed in 1807. The U.S. Congress outlawed the slave trade, but not slavery, a year later. Brazil only finally gave up the slave trade in 1888.

Barbary Corsairs

If conditions were bad on normal pirate boats, you should have seen life in the galleys of the Barbary corsairs. The mostly Muslim pirates caused havoc on the southern coast of Britain in the 1620s. They came from the Barbary Coast seaports of Tunis, Tripoli, Salé, and Algiers and were mostly interested in slaves, particularly in the strong British ones. They'd been given authorization from their leaders to attack anything Christian, so for years they terrorized British beaches and seaside towns, dragging people from their homes and taverns to crew their boats. The corsairs would sometimes capture whole fishing fleets and merchant ships trying to leave the bigger southern ports of Falmouth and Plymouth. At one point, the authorities in Britain even had to smother the Lizard Lighthouse. This famous warning on the southern tip of Britain was turning out to be more use to the Barbary pirates than to British sailors. The corsairs figured that if they kept harassing Britain, in a few years the monarch would have no sailors left.

At the height of their success, the Barbary pirates had at least 20,000 Christians, mostly British, in captivity enduring terrible conditions. The long, narrow Barbary pirate galleys didn't have as many sails as other ships and relied on banks of oars (fifty plus) to propel them along at speeds of up to five miles an hour. This was especially useful when overhauling an enemy ship becalmed by lack of wind.

In the sweltering, stinking galleys, the rowers would be chained naked to their benches, expected to row for up to twenty hours at a time, and were beaten mercilessly if they so much as slowed down, let alone collapsed.★ For food they would be given either a thin gruel or dry bread soaked in water or vinegar. When a galley slave died, as they eventually did, he'd be unceremoniously tossed over the side and a slightly fresher one brought in.

HAVEN'T THEY HEARD OF SAILS?

Many of the captives decided that they might live longer if they converted to Islam. On the good side, as Muslims, they got better conditions and more food but on the downside if captured, they'd be just as likely to be strung up as their new shipmates.

And strung up they were. In 1725 the Barbary pirates were driven from British waters by naval patrols that captured and hanged most of them with great glee.

★ *They had to keep up with the strict drumbeat.*

ROTTEN FOOD
FOR ROTTEN MEN

Probably the very worst thing about being a pirate was the food. It was usually as bad as it can get and far worse than your grandmother's cooking or even the school cafeteria. The problem was always about keeping the food fresh. Instead of having fridges or freezers, pirates were forced to keep their supplies in damp, stinky, dusty, leaky holds, which made food rot as soon as they looked at it. If they wanted meat, they either had to salt it before they left port (salt meat's pretty disgusting anyway), smoke it, or, literally, walk it on board—baaing, oinking, clucking, mooing, and whatever noise goats make. Needless to say, the smell of the animals' quarters was only matched by that of the pirates', who, just like the animals, were not known to wash that often.

Pirates could, of course, catch fish but, as you might have guessed, they were a lazy, impatient bunch and usually couldn't be bothered. (Well, they couldn't be bothered till they absolutely had to be.) When a crew ran out of grub altogether, no creature—be it turtles (or their eggs), penguins, seals (apparently horrible), seagulls, rats, or bats—was completely safe.

RATATOUILLE

Eating ~~With~~ the Captain

It was not completely unknown for the starving crew to send someone down to the hold for one of the plumper slaves whom they'd stolen from some other ship or even captured themselves.

The motley crew of a ship that William Dampier, the British explorer, was sailing with, were the worst rabble imaginable. They once secretly agreed, at a time when they were running a little short in the grub department, that the only thing to do, if the situation got much worse, was to dine on the captain and Dampier—as they were the only two worth eating.

By the Way

Chicken eggs were called cackle-fruit, for obvious reasons.

If pirates hadn't made their living robbing and murdering, they could have called in at all the big ports, like other sailors, but because they were likely to get their necks well stretched if they even tiptoed on the beach, they had to stay away. The only fresh supplies, therefore, had to be stolen from other ships or fishing boats, plundered from small seaside villages, or simply hunted for when ashore.

Anyone for Lime Juice?

Because of their severe lack of vitamin C, due to their dreadful diet (no vegetables or fruit), pirates suffered from a horrid disease called scurvy. In the mid-1700s, it was discovered that citrus fruits, particularly limes, did a lot to prevent this disease and from then on pirates always carried as many as possible on board.

Hardtack

When everything else ran out, the poor old pirates resorted to hardtack, a sort of indigestible cracker made simply from flour and water. After a few weeks at sea, these crackers were usually

infested with big-headed weevil maggots that flourished in the damp, gloomy atmosphere. In fact, the starving men preferred to eat hardtack in the dark. Weevils should definitely be not seen and not heard.

Pirate Recipes

The crew of the seventeenth-century Welsh buccaneer, Sir Henry Morgan became so hungry on one of its longer voyages that the crew resorted to this rather gruesome recipe:

- Take one leather satchel (or anything leathery—shoes, saddles, harnesses, etc.).
- Tenderize by rubbing the large pieces between heavy stones.

- Scrape off the hair from the rough side with a sharp knife.
- Cut into very small bite-sized pieces and add anything you have left for flavoring.
- Add salt and pepper to taste.
- Roast or boil till soft.
- Serve hot to starving crew.

Salmagundi

When food was more plentiful, the pirates (especially the infamous pirate, Blackbeard) had a favorite dish that they always asked for in pirate restaurants. It was called salmagundi. Here's the recipe, should you ever have a buccaneer to breakfast, brunch, or supper:

- Take some or all of the following . . . turtle meat, fish, pork, chicken, corned beef, ham, duck, or pigeon.
- Chop into chunks and roast with cabbage (optional), anchovies, herring, mangoes, hard-boiled eggs, palm hearts, onions, olives, grapes, and anything pickled.
- Add lots of garlic, salt, pepper, and mustard seeds.
- Smother in oil and vinegar.
- Serve with as much rum or beer as your guest can get down his neck.

Indian Fast Food?

I'm not too sure whether this little incident should go in this section, but it is loosely to do with eating, so I'll go for it. Christopher Condent, a British sailor and latter-day pirate, was a quartermaster on a New York merchant sloop. An Indian seaman, fed up with being bullied by the rest of the crew, decided to blow up the ship for revenge. He was just about to light the pile of gunpowder he'd collected, when Condent—cutlass in one hand and pistol in the other—leaped down into the hold. The Indian, quick as a flash, grabbed another pistol and shot Condent, splintering his cutlass arm, but was himself hit in the middle of the head by the only shot that Condent managed to fire off.

The crew were understandably annoyed with the Indian seaman and, as the story goes, "hack'd him to Pieces, and the Gunner ripped up his Belly, tore out his Heart, boiled it and ate it." What the poor soul's heart was doing in his belly we'll never know—or the recipe he used—but I'm pretty sure you won't find it in any books on Indian cooking.

HE'S TOUGHER THAN WE THOUGHT

And Drinks . . .

I bet you could have sold pirates any number of devices that supposedly converted seawater to fresh. Freshwater was a continual headache on pirate ships (or any ships come to that), because it was always stored in dirty old barrels and soon went putrid. Crews took with them as many barrels of beer, wine, brandy, and rum (grog★) as they could carry, and when they ran out of their own they would try their level best to steal it from the ships they overran. And that, dear reader, is one of the main reasons why pirates were nearly always drunk.

★ *Grog, by the way, was watered-down rum.*

Bumboo

Perhaps the favorite drink of all pirates was called bumboo, a mixture of rum and sugar, flavored with nutmeg.

Don't Try This at Home

On the downside, pirates sometimes had to resort to far less attractive drinks. On one occasion, pirate captain Bartholomew Roberts and his crew of 124 men found themselves short of water. They had only sixty-three gallons of water with which to cross the Atlantic Ocean. Due to poor winds, the days dragged into weeks and the weeks months, and the men, driven almost insane with thirst, were down to one mouthful of water a day. In the end, they resorted to drinking seawater or, even worse, their own urine. Many died, but the ones who survived best were those who stuck to their rations. There's a lesson in there somewhere. However thirsty you are, don't ever be tempted to drink your own . . . well, you know what I mean.

EE! I'VE TASTED WORSE

OPTIONAL EXTRA

HANDY HOOK

ESSENTIAL CARTOON PIRATEWEAR

BIG HATS AND BAGGY TROUSERS

Most guys (and girls) think that the sort of stuff they see pirates wearing in the movies is great—big hats, baggy trousers, patches, etc., but the bold buccaneers weren't really as fashionable as they appeared clotheswise. Part of the job, you must realize, involved living in an atmosphere that was sometimes damp, sometimes windy, sometimes freezing, and sometimes blisteringly hot. Not only that but they were constantly being doused in saltwater. All of these things, plus the stray bullet hole or knife slash, have a tendency to make your clothes wear out quickly. Most times, however, they simply rotted off the bold buccaneers' backs.

GOSH- A BARE BUCCANEER

This, as you might imagine, was a huge headache for your average pirate, because he usually only possessed the clothes he stood up in. Therefore, next to a good supply of grog and a worthwhile haul of trinkets every now and then, clothes, which were very expensive before the nineteenth century (mass manufacture and all that), became extremely precious.

What Shall I Wear Today?

Not a common question below decks. All seamen from the 1500s who *weren't* in the British navy wore the same sort of outfit—baggy canvas trousers, called slops, cut off halfway down the calf (often made from worn out sails), a bright neckerchief (sometimes worn around the head), and a heavy, loose-fitting woolen shirt belted at the waist. Pirates often plastered their clothes with black tar to preserve them from the elements. This, as you can imagine, made them smell and feel terrible. Worse still, pirates wore no underwear and only occasionally washed their clothes in seawater, so you can imagine just how smelly and itchy they became after only a couple of weeks at sea.

By the Way

I bet you can't guess why pirates nearly always wore a large golden earring. It was so that if they ever drowned after a shipwreck,

there'd be enough money to give them a decent burial (if their bodies turned up, that is).

Shoe-Free Zone

Ordinary pirates didn't generally like shoes. Firstly they usually couldn't afford them, having spent all their money on booze and gambling. Secondly, bare feet gave better grip on a deck covered in water (or—on a good day—blood), and were more practical for shinning up ropes, monkey fashion. Also, it must be said, the pirates did occasionally eat them if they became really desperate.

In the Mediterranean, where it got very hot, it was not unusual for the pirate crew to dispense with clothes altogether and swing about the rigging completely naked.

Time to Dress Up

When the pirate captains, surgeons, or quartermasters went ashore, they generally put on a kind of long, knee-length, brass-buttoned tunic, which they belted around the waist over long stockings or even tights. On their heads would be the famous tricorn hat and on their feet the highly fashionable, large-buckled, tallish-heeled shoes or boots.

During the sixteenth century, sailors usually wore slops. When they went ashore, they simply wore a tunic over them or tucked it into their slops like a shirt.

In those days, the captains often didn't look much more fashionable than anyone else when aboard ship, but whenever they went anywhere remotely special they dressed up to look like gentry, so everyone would know who they were dealing with. Most pirate captains insisted on wearing these magnificent clothes when they went into battle, and some even put them on when they were about to be hanged.

Ruff Trade

In the 1500s, the time of Sir Francis Drake and Sir Walter Raleigh, a captain (even a pirate captain) would wear clothes consisting of breeches tied with colored ribbons around the knees, a padded doublet, heavily embroidered and with a scattering of jewels, one of those frilly collars around the neck, a voluminous cloak, and all of this finished off with a cocked hat with a big, brightly colored feather sticking out of it.

Just about everyone in those days had a beard and moustache (even some of the women, I wouldn't mind betting). Ordinary sailors would have their hair pulled back to keep it out of their eyes and plaited into a tarry pigtail. Pirates seldom cut their hair and were only forced to do so when it became inhabited by stowaway lice.

Seventeenth-Century Pirate Wear

In the 1600s, they still had the same baggy slops down to just below the knee, but this time with woollen stockings and a long shirt or coat. It was during this period that the extremely sissy-looking petticoat trousers became popular, especially with the captains. These looked like long, knee-length, wide-at-the-bottom divided skirts. The reason you don't see any of these outfits in pirate films is most likely because the directors don't want their heroes (or villains come to that) looking too girlish.

DARN. I'VE GOT A RUN IN ME STOCKING!

Cross-Dressing?

Talking of looking girlish, it was well recorded that when the rough and ragged pirates attacked a ship with ladies aboard, before doing anything else, they would rip off the poor damsels' clothes. Not, I must stress, to ogle at their naked bodies, or even to have their wicked way with them (that wasn't allowed)—but to steal their dresses. It was not that unusual to see a filthy, long-haired, tattooed, fully armed, macho pirate leaping around the deck wearing the latest in seventeenth-century high-court ladies' fashions.

SICK AS A PARROT

So here you have a relatively small ship in a relatively huge ocean inhabited by a relatively unruly bunch of shipmates. They not only didn't bathe properly, but didn't eat or drink well either. As a result, your bold buccaneer tended to be liable for just about every disgusting disease going. Not only that, but a lot of seamen picked up some very unpleasant illnesses from the brothels in ports visited on their travels.

WHO ARE YOU CALLING AN UNPLEASANT THING

And it wouldn't be down to the sickroom, where a nice nurse would tend to their every need—oh no! If your average pirate woke up feeling a little under the weather, there was a strong chance that he'd end up going over the side as fish food, for there was no such thing as a doctor aboard a pirate

ship (unless they'd captured one) let alone a nurse, and little in the way of medicine.

Sicknesswise, some places were worse than others. The pirates who hung around Europe and the cooler areas weren't at half the risk as those who sailed the tropics—those seas around the scorching, mosquito-infested coasts of Africa. Just as an example, seamen on the slave ships that plied the waters between Africa and the West Indies threw the corpses of four to five slaves overboard daily, as well as a fair proportion of their shipmates. It was much the same on the pirate ships. By the time a voyage was over, it was not unheard of for your average hardworking pirate to lose up to 40 percent of his friends.

So what were the main diseases?

Scurvy

Scurvy and seafaring men go together like dogs and fleas. This disease is reckoned to have killed 200,000 seamen between 1500 and 1900. The problem was dietary. Sailors didn't seem to realize that a human being needs fruits and vegetables to keep reasonably healthy. Even if they had realized it, however, in those days on board ship there was no way of keeping produce from rotting after more than a couple of days.

When your mom and dad tell you that you must eat your vegetables, they're not kidding (they're probably not pirates either, but we won't go into that). Scurvy is a nasty disease that results from a diet that includes no fruits or vegetables and therefore no vitamin C.

Symptoms

Loss of appetite, pale skin with dark blotches, spongy pimply gums that bleed easily, teeth falling out, swelling of the legs, roughness of the skin, diarrhea (even more unpleasant on a small ship with no bathrooms), awful lethargy, and a certain loss of vision. If you happen to have all these symptoms, might I suggest you go immediately to your local store and buy lots of lemons, limes, or oranges and suck 'em dry. It has been said that the symptoms will miraculously clear up in a couple of days—mine did!

Interesting Fact?
British sailors were called limeys because, after 1795, the Royal Navy provided fresh lime juice on all voyages. The British merchant navy followed in 1854. (The U.S. Navy didn't catch on until World War II.)

Yellow Fever
One of the bad things about living in and around a hot sunny climate like you get in Africa and the Caribbean is that you are far more likely to catch a horrid and scary disease called yellow fever. It was first "discovered" by the infamous sixteenth-century Spanish conquistadors when they conquered South America, and many say it served them right. You can lay the blame for us humans catching yellow fever fairly and squarely at the feet (all six of 'em) of your common mosquito and the forest monkeys from whom the skeeter picks up the disease.

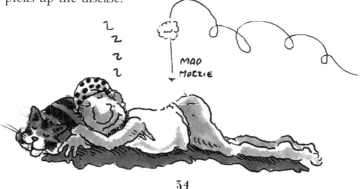

MAD MOZZIE

These days you'd be inoculated against it, but that option didn't exist around the seventeenth century. So if, in the middle of the night, your potential target pirate was to have a skeeter visitor, there was a fair chance that, providing the little varmint was carrying the disease, he'd get the full works. Which were:

Symptoms

For the first few days after being bitten, the patient could take it easy while the virus spread and multiplied throughout his body (yuck!). Then, suddenly, he'd get a chronic headache, backache, start being sick everywhere, and then he'd get hotter and hotter and HOTTER. After three long, sweat-pouring, hallucinating days of utter agony, his fever would go either of two ways. It could be:

Good News: The patient would start to recover fully and, even better, be immune from yellow fever for the rest of his life.

OR

Bad News: He'd get progressively worse for three days, until he vomited black blood (ugh!) and then there wouldn't be any rest of his life. I suppose it wasn't all bad news; after all, he couldn't get the disease again either, could he?

Dysentery

Dysentery is a horrible disease and almost too yucky to talk about. You get it when a lot of people are crowded together, don't wash their hands after going to the bathroom, and then handle food. On a pirate ship, not only did they not have proper toilets (with soap dispensers and sinks, etc.), but the water was far too precious to be used for washing. Actually pirates were a filthy bunch who wouldn't have washed their hands anyway.

Symptoms

Don't worry, you'll soon know if you've got it: severe bouts of blood-filled diarrhea, followed by severe stomach pains, followed by a severe thirst, followed by, if you're a bit unlucky, severe death. Severely not to be recommended.

Medical Tip

If you've got dysentery, don't, for God's sake, confuse it with scurvy for, if you rush for the fruit bowl, it'll more than likely make it much worse.

Psittacosis (Parrot Disease)

Talk about "sick as a parrot." This is where the term comes from. Psittacosis is a nasty little disease of birds (particularly

SICK PARROT

parrots), which is easily transmitted to humans (particularly pirates). The joke is that the birds don't have that much of a bad time with the disease, but humans get it much worse (if you call dying much worse).

How to Catch it

Easy! Go to your parrot's cage, put your head through the door, and sniff the bottom (of the cage, not the parrot). Psittacosis is caught from inhaling the dust of dried-out parrot poop.

Symptoms

The patient starts climbing on people's shoulders, flapping his arms about, and copying everything they say at the top of his voice. Actually, that's a lie—it's worse than that. Someone with psittacosis suffers from an extremely high temperature of a hundred and something, followed by pneumonia, severe weakness, and really fast breathing. It lasts two to three weeks after which time he either gets better . . . or he doesn't!

By the Way

Pirates really did have parrots as pets, not always because they wanted them, but because the pesky peckers would often follow the pirate ships when they left their desert islands thinking there'd be more to eat. Often they'd be lucky if the pirates didn't eat them.

Injury Time

These days, if we hurt ourselves, we either search for a bandage, swallow an antibiotic or, if it's something more serious, call an ambulance and rush to the nearest hospital where a fully trained staff will figure out what's wrong (if you don't mind waiting). In the seventeenth century, there were no such things as hospitals, skilled surgeons, or drugs like antibiotics to combat infection. And that was on land! Ships, and especially pirate ships, were much, much worse, and so were the sorts of injuries pirates were likely to suffer. I mean, when did you last get hit on the back of the head by a cannon ball or have your arm lopped off by a cutlass?

Admittedly, on board ship, one of the crew would usually be delegated to tend to the injured. But his equipment would be primitive, to say the least, and although he'd more than likely have his own sharp knives (essential pirate gear), for major operations like amputations he'd simply borrow a saw from the ship's carpenter—if indeed he wasn't the ship's carpenter.

Anesthetic? Forget it. The patient would probably be filled up with rum or brandy until sloshed to the point of oblivion. This same alcohol would then be poured on the open wound in a vain effort to ward off festering, but often with little effect. One of the only ways of being sure of stopping the infection was to put a lighted ember or red hot iron to the injury (this was called cauterizing), but the patient had a nasty habit of dying from the treatment, which was kind of counterproductive. There is absolutely no doubt that most of the seamen who underwent any form of surgery on pirate ships would have died from either the shock or the infection that followed. In fact, those guys hobbling around on wooden legs could be regarded as the lucky ones.

THAT'S REALLY LUCKY

Gangrene

Gangrene not only sounds disgusting, it is! It's a horrible disease that results from the infection that sets in after a severe wound or burn. This would have been the usual cause of death to most pirates after a battle at sea. The flesh actually begins to rot (especially in hot weather), owing to a lack of blood supply. The smell, as you can imagine . . . is—er—unimaginable. The only thing you can do is to keep cutting back behind the gangrene in the hope that the wound won't re-infect, but you can end up with no limb at all—which is a bit tricky if you're a pirate.

An Eye for an Eye

Pirates were very aware of the dangers of so much fighting and a proportion of any stolen haul was set aside by the quartermaster to compensate the men for any serious injury received in battle. It went like this:

- Worst of all was the loss of a right arm—the cutlass arm. For that, if he survived, he could expect 600 pieces of eight (Spanish dollars).
- The other arm or either leg came in slightly less at 500 pieces.
- A lost eye was worth 100 pieces of eight (which would buy a lot of black patches), but I suppose it's fair to surmise the loss of both would have been considerably more than double. Let's face it, there are better things to be than a pirate if you can't see.

Malaria

Anyone or anything can and could catch malaria—birds, monkeys, lizards, hamsters, pirates—and, of course, us. Just like yellow fever, it is carried by mosquitoes, but this time, there's sixty different types of the disease to choose from. Four of these affect humans: *Plasmodium vivax*, which causes the sufferer to have a fever every other day (only half as bad); *Plasmodium malariae,* which takes a long time to appear and causes fever every three days (only a third as bad); and the last two, *Plasmodium ovale,* which is mild, and *Plasmodium falciparum.* This last one gives you jungle fever and causes coma and madness and kills you pretty quickly by blocking the blood vessels to the brain (not that pirates had much brain to run blood vessels to).

Cure?

Ah, here lies the problem. Malaria is usually treated with quinine, a drug obtained from the bark of the cinchona tree. This is fine except the tree only grows in the Andean highlands of Peru—a slight problem if you're stuck in a boat miles from anywhere.

Consumption (Tuberculosis)

Very popular among those who live and work in cold, damp conditions with very poor food (in other words—pirate ships). This tricky little disease has a bad habit of lying around in the body for as long as it feels like before it decides to zap you. In fact, a quarter of us have the bacillus *Mycobacterium tuberculosis* lurking around inside us without our ever knowing.

Symptoms

Obviously, this sneaky disease shows no symptoms in the early stages (otherwise you'd know you had it), but after a while the patient starts feeling tired, feverish, loses his appetite, and begins to lose weight. Then, if it's the worst kind, he starts having chest pains and coughs up blood. If he doesn't get taken immediately to a hospital (which again is difficult if rocking about on the high seas) and isn't given a massive dose of antibiotics (not invented in those days), he usually dies—which most pirates had a habit of doing.

PUNISHING PIRATES

Almost all British pirates had at one time or another been in the Royal Navy or on merchant vessels—not by choice, but because they'd been "pressed" into it. The press-gang was feared by every hard-drinking man in every tavern in every port in the world. When a captain was a bit short in the old crew department for a particular voyage, he'd send out a bunch of his roughest, toughest men. Late in the evening, when most of the men in the taverns would be as drunk as parrots, the press-gang would grab as many as he needed. By the time the poor souls sobered up, it would be too late, they'd be at sea, and the only way back would be to swim.

By the Way

When a man joined the Royal Navy in those days, he'd receive a shilling from the king (rotten deal!). When a kidnapped seaman awoke aboard ship, he would find a shilling "pressed" in his hand. This was a slick trick to prove he'd agreed willingly.

Once at sea, that's when the trouble started. Discipline on board for your average seaman could be incredibly cruel. Disobedience could be punished in many ways. Sailors could be forced to swallow cockroaches, have their teeth knocked out, or have iron bolts screwed into their mouths so they'd choke on their own blood. Almost worst of all, they could be flogged by a frayed, tarred rope called a cat-o'-nine-tails while tied to the mainmast. Sometimes a man could be flogged over 500 times, and sometimes, just to add a little spice to the proceedings, the flogger would customize his whip by knotting the ends or adding musket balls or even fish hooks (ouch!). Then, if the floggee had been really disobedient, they'd rub salt and vinegar into his raw flesh after the event—guaranteed to make the poor fellow's eyes water even more.

Anyone for Keelhauling?

Then there was always keelhauling, the horrendous punishment by which the guilty party was dragged under and across the bottom of the ship by a rope so that the barnacles scraped his skin off—a punishment that was often fatal, especially if the victim got a severe nibbling by sharks.

All this for only a few bucks a month!

By the Way

In 1790 a lot of the worst punishments on British ships were banned when the Articles of War were published. (The articles were a serious and specific set of laws that all British sailors were expected to live by.)

Pirate Punishments

You could still be punished on pirate ships, but it generally wasn't quite so sadistic. Here are just a few examples:

Man Overboard

If a pirate was found guilty of a serious crime against another man, he'd either be thrown over the side and not thought of again or towed behind the ship on a length of rope until he was either dead from hypothermia (the cold), exhaustion, boredom, or simply drowning.

Marooning

If a crime wasn't quite so bad, but bad nonetheless, the pirates went in for marooning— that is, leaving the poor fellow on some remote, deserted island. Or they might set him adrift on just a tiny raft, with no clothes and no provisions (unless you count a gun to kill himself with if things started to look too dire). This was the punishment for anything approaching mutiny or threatening the captain.

Dunking

At suppertime this was quite often done to the hardtack to soften it and slightly less often to pirates who wouldn't do as they were told. They would lower the stubborn pirate over and over into the ocean and, in between, hang him up to dry in the blazing sun. Very good, as it happens, for the old suntan, but the victim very often ended up rather overdone.

Rules is Rules

Everyone thinks that being a pirate for a living meant that you didn't have to do all the stuff that real sailors had to do—wear pressed uniforms, brush your teeth, obey orders, bathe every night, not answer back to the captain, etc. But that was sometimes far from the truth. As you might imagine, having anything up to a couple of hundred rough, tough criminals on one ship could create a few problems. Pirates often had a strict set of rules to follow, and if they broke them, there'd be painful results.

Things Pirates Couldn't Do

Oddly enough, most pirate ships had a strict code of conduct, and this was often on display for all to see (and for all to sign). There were a few things that they just couldn't do— things like:

No Girls

Attempting to sneak women aboard, keeping them below decks, or even disguising them as regular seamen were all forbidden. If pirates were found to be doing this, the punishment was short and swift. They were either flung over the side (often in shark–infested waters), hung from the yard-arm, or simply run through with the captain's sword.

Often pirates would be sailing for months or even years at a time. When they'd hit the seaports, they'd typically seek out brothels (whorehouses),

CAUSE AND EFFECT

where they often caught horrendous incurable diseases from the ladies of easy virtue.

It was forbidden to meddle with women of good birth from a captured ship. Penalty—DEATH. (It's usually thought that if pirates captured a ship, whatever was on board was theirs for the taking—including any women. Although they were generally allowed to have their will with the slaves and servant girls, they were strictly forbidden to ravage any of the high-born women—probably because the captain wanted them for himself!)

No Stealing
Anyone who stole anything over the value of a piece of eight (there was no such thing as a piece of seven) would be marooned on a desert island.

No Secrets
If a man tried to keep a big secret from the other pirates, he'd be sent away on a little raft with a small pistol, some powder, some shot, and a bottle of water if he was lucky.

No Violence
Any man who struck another on board and injured him could expect old Moses' eye-for-an-eye law—in this case thirty-nine lashes on his bare back.

No Dirty Weapons
If a man was found with a dirty weapon, if he was not ready at all times for service, or if he didn't do enough work around the place, he would forfeit his share of any stolen goods.

No Danger
If a man let off his musket for a laugh, or smoked his pipe down in the hold, or carried a candle without a cover, he also lost his share of any loot.

It Could Only Happen to Pirates (avoid this part if you're at all squeamish)

After all that stuff about the sort of treatment that sent sailors to become pirates, you might want to hear of some of the things they did to others when *they* were calling the shots.

Ups and Downs

When the British captain, William Snelgrave, was captured by pirates in 1719, he was forced to watch what they did to a French captain who'd been captured just before him. The pirates tied a rope round his neck and hoisted him up into the sails over and over again until he became unconscious. Another favorite was to stuff oakum (the tarry rope used for sealing the gaps between the ship's planks) into the mouths of their victims and then set fire to it.

No Sweat

A great pirate laugh was called "sweating," a fun little event in which the pirates would strip their victim and, to the tune of the ship's fiddler, force him to run around and around the mizzenmast by sticking him in the backside with knives, forks, harpoons, or anything sharp they could get their hands

on—until he collapsed from exhaustion. If the pirates felt that wasn't enough, they sometimes put the exhausted man into a barrel full of cockroaches who would gorge themselves on his blood. Nice!

Musical Cannons

There's a picture in *The Pirates* by Douglas Botting of two pirates in the year 1718 careering around the deck on the backs of a couple of Portuguese monks, whipping their steeds until the losers collapsed.

Woolding

You should have seen "woolding"—the old pirate method of finding out where the valuables were hidden. This sounds pretty innocent—like something you do to sheep—but it involved tying the victim's arms and legs with rope and stretching him while at the same time beating him with all kinds of implements. Then, just so he didn't get too cozy, he would have burning matches inserted between his fingers, or slender cords twisted about his head until his eyes burst out of his skull. I did warn you!

Barbecue Time

Sir Henry Morgan, who became the governor of Jamaica after a long career privateering, always made out he'd been pretty nice to his prisoners. Oh yeah! Not according to reports of what he did to the women of Portobelo when he captured the port in 1668. Apparently he threw them live onto a baking stove until well done, and all because he thought they had money, which of course they'd denied.

Blow Up

Then there were the buccaneers who tortured Dona Agustin de Rojas, probably the most important woman in Portobelo. She was stripped naked and forced into an empty wine barrel. The barrel was then filled all around her with gunpowder and a pirate held a lighted taper, far too close for comfort, while demanding the whereabouts of her valuables.

Around the Mast

But that was nothing! French pirate chief Montbars of Languedoc figured out a punishment all of his very own. Are you ready for this? He would slit open his victim's stomach and remove one end of his large intestine and nail it to a post. So far not so good. He would then force the victim to dance around and around the post by beating him with a burning spar until his guts (all twenty-five feet of them) were played out and he expired. Phew!

Sorry, folks, but even I can't describe what Captain Morgan's men did to the Portuguese after capturing Gibraltar, but it made the things that I've already described seem like a trip around Disneyland.

LADIES AT SEA

Don't go thinking there were only men out there on the high seas. Okay, being a pirate was generally thought of as a man's job, but there were several well-known female buccanesses throughout history. This is all the more amazing because most of the time women weren't allowed anywhere near pirate ships (unless they were captives or slaves).

All the famous women pirates had originally crept on board dressed as boys and, strange as it may seem, managed to hide their gender from their macho shipmates for quite a while. This was more difficult than you might think. All the guys on board the ships of the seventeenth and eighteenth centuries used to sleep together, eat together, use the same bathroom, and, much more to the point, bathe together—usually from a tub of water and usually on deck in front of everyone. More crucial than that, in hot weather pirates would often charge around in no clothes at all.

It might have escaped your notice, but men and women have a habit of being slightly different physically. Couple that with having no Adam's apple, no five o'clock stubble, no hairy chest—not to mention having a much higher voice, and it all becomes mystifying, to say the very least, how the women were never spotted.

Here are a few lady pirates who not only got away with it, but were eventually able to be recognized for who they really were.

Anne Bonny

Anne Bonny was born in Ireland in the late seventeenth century. She was the illegitimate daughter of a well-known Cork lawyer named William Cormac. His wife kicked him out of the house when she discovered that he'd been having an affair with the maid (who ended up in prison on a false robbery charge). Little Anne was the result of their "indiscretion".

Cormac, as it happens, was very fond of his daughter and decided that he'd like her to come and live with him, but he couldn't admit that she was actually his. He made out, therefore, that she was a boy and that he was simply training "him" as a clerk. To cut the story short, it all came out, and Anne's dad, along with Anne and the maid (now out of jail), sailed to America to start a new life.

But Anne was a wild child with a real sense of adventure and a talent for boxing, of all things. She got together with and married a young trainee pirate called James Bonny and together they sailed to the Bahamas to look for trouble. To cut the short story even shorter, she fell out with her husband and fell in with the swashbuckling "Calico" Jack Rackham, a much-hunted pirate captain. With him she stole a ship and started her true pirate career. But, as I said earlier, pirate ships didn't allow women, let alone wives, on board, so Anne simply reverted to what she knew best and masqueraded as a man again.

Mary Read

Mary Read was born in Britain toward the end of the seventeenth century. Due to a little misunderstanding, her mother's husband had run off to sea before Mary was born, leaving Mary's mother with a young son. Her mother then became pregnant again almost immediately by someone else and, just before the baby (Mary) was born, the son died (so far so bad). Then, to avoid admitting to an illegitimate child and so as to get money off her runaway husband's rich parents, Mary's mother moved away and made out that Mary was the baby boy who had died. From then on, therefore, Mary had to be male. Clear so far?

At thirteen, Mary got a job in a big London house as a footboy not a maid. But she found this boring and also ran away to sea like her mother's old husband, still dressed as a boy. After this, she joined the army, but carelessly fell in love with a boy (there's always a catch somewhere), who, as you might imagine, at first thought her behavior kind of strange until Mary revealed her true identity.

Anyway, they left the army and started a pub together, but hubby carelessly died. In 1697 Mary, who wasn't really cut out for pub life, put on men's clothes once more, became a soldier again, and was posted to the West Indies. Guess what? The ship was captured by pirates and our Mary found herself in the same crew with Rackham and the other man/woman—Anne Bonny. Oh dear, oh dear, Anne Bonny found herself attracted to the dashing young "man," and eventually it became necessary for Mary and Anne to "compare notes," so to speak. Anne then confessed all to her husband Calico Jack Rackham, who told them both, for heaven's sake, to keep the fact that they were women under their hats (and their shirts). But then Mary suddenly fell for a fellow pirate and revealed all.

The two women, always dressed as men, were a formidable team, however. And were every bit as fierce and fearless as the rest of the crew. In 1720, after a short career of severe swashbuckling, when anchored off the island of Jamaica, Rackham and his merry men (and two women) were suddenly attacked by a British naval sloop. Rackham and the men were below decks lying around in a drunken stupor after a heavy night, so the two women fought the navy single-handedly with anything they could lay their hands on. They were magnificent. Eventually, however, when even *they* realized the game was up, they turned on their shipmates, who were now hiding below, calling them all cowards and killing and injuring several.

When Rackham and the rest of the crew were finally executed in Jamaica, Mary and Anne, also accused of "Piracies, Felonies, and Robberies . . . on the High Sea," were found guilty but got off on a technicality. While awaiting trial, they cleverly wheedled themselves into pregnancy, and it was the rule in those days that pregnant women could not be hanged—neat, eh?

By the Way

Just to prove what a toughie Anne Bonny was, when visiting her husband Calico Jack waiting for execution, she told him that she was admittedly sorry to see him in such a predicament but that if he'd fought like a man, he wouldn't be about to be hanged like a dog (who hangs dogs anyway, I ask myself?).

And later?

Mary died shortly after, before the birth of her baby, having caught the dreaded yellow fever in jail. It was rumored that Anne's wealthy dad (remember him?) bought his daughter's release.

Grace O'Malley

If you're one of those people who's interested in buried treasure and stuff like that, you might be interested in Grace O'Malley, the sixteenth-century Irish piratess who apparently buried nine tons of it. But before you go out with your bucket and shovel, beware . . . Old Grace apparently laid a nasty curse on anyone who should happen to find it. (Mean or what?)

Grace O'Malley came from the mighty and powerful O'Malley family, which had forts and castles all over the western coast of Ireland, as well as a huge fleet of pirate ships. Grace, by the way, when a little girl, was horribly scarred on the face by the beak and talons of a naughty eagle, whom she was trying to dissuade from carrying off her daddy's lambs.

Anyway, Mr. O'Malley trained his daughter to be a brave warrior(ess), and, when he died, she took over as leader of the terrifying O'Malley pirates, who caused havoc all along the coast of Ireland. So much so that Queen Elizabeth I, who ruled England from 1558 to 1603, offered the equivalent of $120,000 for her capture.

Grace really was some girl by all accounts, and there are hundreds of legends and stories about her bravery. Apparently, when she was a young mother (her son was one day old), she helped repel some Muslim pirates who were attacking her ship. Her captain supposedly came below to report that they were getting the worst of it. Grace cursed her crew and rushed onto the deck with a musket in one hand and presumably the baby in the other shouting and screaming fit

to frighten the very bravest Muslim.

Later, when sixty years old, she attacked a Spanish vessel just off the coast of Ireland, this time crashing onto the deck in her nightie, waving her pistols, and looking fierce in her curlers and all. The poor Spaniards thought Grace was a crazed ghost and surrendered without firing a shot.

By the Way

As a caring parent, it must be said, the old girl left a lot to be desired. Legend has it that on one occasion her poor son fell overboard while they were on their way home after a few weeks' persistent pirating. He eventually struggled to the side of the boat and grabbed at it, but his mother chopped off his hand, leaving him to die in the waves claiming that had he been a true O'Malley, he wouldn't have fallen over in the first place. A hard way to learn a lesson, I'd have thought! Grace was eventually captured but, after an eighteen-month stretch in a Limerick jail, soon returned to her old tricks again. In the meantime, her hubbie had died. In those days, a wife had no right to her husband's lands, so Grace found herself alone and vulnerable. Instead of waiting to be attacked by her hostile neighbors, old Grace attacked them first. She was captured yet again, and this time her whole fleet was confiscated. But Grace appealed to Queen Elizabeth as one woman to another, claiming she'd been forced into it. Queen Liz rather liked the eccentric old girl and ordered her captors to figure it all out, to give Grace a break, and to let her live the rest of her life in comfort and peace. The old pirate died aged seventy-three in 1603, and one of her brave sons went on to become Viscount Mayo.

THANKS A LOT MOMO

Mrs. Cheng

To be honest, there were quite a few girl/boys like the ones I've just mentioned, but you couldn't really beat the infamous Chinese pirate chief Cheng I Sao. Mrs. Cheng, as she was known, was a Chinese prostitute from

Yo Ho Ho

Canton (now called Guangzhou) and the widow of Cheng I who'd controlled all the sea between Hong Kong and Vietnam. They ruled an army of the most bloodthirsty pirates ever to sail the seven seas.

Nothing was safe from Mr. and Mrs. Cheng. They even ran a protection racket for the smaller merchant ships, which they couldn't be bothered to plunder, as well as all the little fishing vessels that operated in the same waters. The merchants were forced to pay fees at a series of collection posts along the coast.

Mr. Cheng died violently in 1807, and his wife promptly appointed Chang Pao, a brilliant buccaneer whom her husband had once captured and later adopted, to command what she called the Red Flag Fleet. She had an affair with him and later married him. While Mrs. Cheng remained the total boss, Chang became in charge of operations.

Their house (or boat) rules were even stricter than those of the Caribbean pirates and went along these lines:

1) Rape of women prisoners was punished by death, but if—and here's the rub—the woman in question had agreed to it, it was still off with the head for the man, and over the side for the woman (with a heavy weight tied to her ankles).

2) For disobeying orders or stealing any of the treasure before it was shared, instant beheading.

3) Desertion or absence without leave was met with a severe loss in the ear department (both were chopped off).

4) If plundered goods were concealed, it was a whipping of the worst order, and on a second offense—it was severe head removal again (well not actually again, but you know what I mean).

Mrs. Cheng became so powerful that even the Chinese army and navy couldn't get near her. She had nearly 400 oceangoing junks, larger than many a countrys' navy and at times up to 7,000 men. And, oh boy, was she cruel. At one time in 1809, her boys attacked a village that had helped her enemies, and took horrible revenge. They burned it to the ground and beheaded its eighty male inhabitants, hanging their heads on a large banyan tree as a warning to others. The women and children were dragged off to the boats to be done with as Mrs. Cheng saw fit.

In the end, the Chinese asked for the help of the British and Portuguese navies. But even that didn't work—the pirates were just too powerful. So the Chinese government offered Cheng and Chang an amnesty (basically if they promised to be good right away, they'd be free from prosecution).

Mrs. Cheng and Chang Pao liked the idea and settled down in Canton, where the former opened a Chinese restaurant—no she didn't, she opened a massive gambling house and died, aged sixty-nine, an immensely rich old lady.

PIRATE FUN

Being a pirate wasn't all about capturing treasure ships, swigging grog, counting treasure, and stuff like that. Much of the time was spent lounging around on deck, desperate for something to come over the horizon that they could attack. Pirate ships, if you think about it, weren't often actually going anywhere, so they'd loiter around the trade routes waiting for ships that actually were. Sometimes they could hang around for months and therefore had to amuse themselves as best they could. Here are a few of the things they got up to:

Heads You Win

Pirates loved to gamble with cards, dice, or even who they were going to capture next. In fact, gambling was almost as popular as drinking (well almost). One of the problems was that pirates being pirates, they could get completely carried away and lose all their property, not to mention the clothes they stood up in or even their wives back home. And, almost inevitably, just like in the cowboy films, it would all end in a massive fight. Many captains, like privateer Woodes Rogers, actually had to ban gambling of any kind on board his ship, the *Duke*. He made everyone, right down to the cabin boy's parrot, sign a document, in case they changed their minds.

PIRATE PANTS

Some captains who didn't actually ban gambling were often able to use the sailors' inability to control their weakness to their advantage. You see, the trouble with big pirate ships (just like small kids) had always been that when the crew wanted to go ashore for fun and games, someone had to stay behind to look after the ship. Obviously all those who had lost their hard-fought-for money had to stay aboard, while the others hit the town.

Mock Trials

Most pirates, despite being a bloodthirsty lot, were pretty scared of the prospect of what would happen to them if they ever got caught—a quickish trial, a tallish gibbet, and a longish rope—and that's if they were lucky! It became quite common to act out a mock trial, a weird kind of pantomime where everyone aboard dressed up for his part. The captain was usually the judge, and the rest of the crew would play the lawyers, the jury, the jailer and, would you believe it, the hangman. In this way, they were able to make light of their almost inevitable fate—to spit in its face, so to speak.

DID ANYONE PACK THE SCRABBLE?

These trials were often acted out with such reality that the poor accused (usually not the brightest member of the crew) became genuinely scared for his life. On one occasion in 1717, a young pirate got himself so wound up that he thought his fellow shipmates really were going to hang him. He lost the plot so badly, in fact, that he threw a homemade grenade at the mock jury and then drew his cutlass and hacked off the arm of the guy acting as the prosecuting lawyer—a pirate who went by the name of Alexander the Great (from then on presumably, Alexander the One-Armed Great).

Party Time

Every time pirates overhauled a ship, they'd have a wild party when they got back to their own boat. As we've already established, they loved to imbibe and were crazy about drinking toasts to just about anyone they could think of— their wives, mistresses, friends, parrots, shipmates, past conquests, future conquests—you name it. Some of the most popular toasts were to God or the Devil, or death to any of a whole gaggle of judges, naval captains, or even royalty who were after their greasy necks. It is said that on the pirate island of Madagascar in the Indian Ocean the speciality was to mix gunpowder with the rum for specially solemn oaths and toasts. Madagascar, by the way, was almost exclusively a pirate island from the 1680s right into the eighteenth century, and many of the leaders had private armies surrounding their massive fortresslike houses.

There were, in fact, many pirate havens where like-minded villains could relax and party to their heart's content with their feet firmly on dry land. The pirates tended to favor tricky little harbors into which huge ships couldn't follow them. The ports—places like Tortuga Island near Hispaniola, New Providence Island in the Bahamas, the Juan Fernández Islands near Chile, Devil's Island off northern South America, and Ocracoke Island on the North Carolina coast—were chosen by their nearness to the trade routes and their faraway-ness from the powers that were out to get them. But their real favorites were the corrupt ports that operated outside the law and actually encouraged the pirates' lucrative business—Port Royal in Jamaica, Algiers on the North African coast, and Fort Dauphine on Madagascar, for example.

Pirate Music

Music was essential to keep pirates' spirits up. Most naval and merchant captains would insist on a ship's band or even a small orchestra. There's no reason to suppose that pirate ships didn't do the same. We know, for instance, that one of the most-prized treasures to be removed from a conquered ship (after the carpenter and the surgeon) would be anyone who could play a musical instrument like a fiddle or a squeeze-box.

These musicians often didn't mind being captured that much, because without doubt, their duties on a pirate ship would be much lighter. And let's face it, being captured was an almost watertight defense if they ever came to trial.

Music While You Work

There would be music while the crew ate their supper, scrubbed the deck, spliced the main brace, shivered their timbers, and most evenings before bedtime. And then there were the dances.

YOU DANCE DIVINELY!

Pirates loved to dance and thought nothing of getting up and dancing with each other to the hornpipe or jig. Best of all, the ship's band would play rousing battle songs while the rest of the pirates were chasing and attacking other boats— banging drums and crashing cymbals and generally making a god-awful noise simply to scare the wits out of their prospective victims.

Many of the pirates' shanties are far too crude to share here, and they mostly boast about pirate exploits not only when fighting but with the opposite sex. Others were sad, whiney laments about their sweethearts back home or what was going to happen to them if they ever got caught.

THE PICK OF THE BUNCH

There were thousands of pirates terrorizing the seven seas during the seventeenth and eighteenth centuries, but some stood out head and shoulders above the rest. Here's the pick of the best—or worst—of 'em!

Blackbeard—The Weirdest

Blackbeard was the nickname given to a dangerous guy named Edward Teach, who was born in Bristol, England, sometime in the late seventeenth century. In a way, he was a failed sailor who turned lawbreaker because he wasn't getting anywhere in the Royal Navy. Nonetheless, he gained a reputation as one of the most terrifying of all pirates and is still more talked about than any of the famous naval captains of the day. Here are just a few of the stories about the old devil.

Appearance

Not content with being fierce, Blackbeard had to *look* fierce as well. He had a good start, for he was built like a wrestler with a horribly twisted nose and big ears. He added to this by sporting a huge, shaggy beard (black obviously), which he  wore in filthy ringlets. To set all this off, Blackbeard would wear a black wide-brimmed pirate hat pulled down right to his eyes. Best of all, when in fighting mode, he would weave hemp cords soaked in saltpeter and limewater into his hair and beard and light them. In doing so, he'd surround his massive head with an eerie glow and thick black smoke.

His demonic appearance was accompanied by a shoulder belt of pistols ready for action and a waist belt with even more pistols and various dangerous-looking daggers and cutlasses. Not someone you'd want to meet on a dark night in a small boat, I'll wager.

Fun and Games

In order to show his crew who was boss, Blackbeard would think up crazy tests of bravery and endurance. Like creating a "hell" of his very own, which he did by challenging his toughest sailors to accompany him down below, where he battened down all the hatches and lit pots of lethal brimstone. As the choking yellow fumes filled the pirates' parlor, one by one the crew dashed on deck gasping in the fresh air, while Blackbeard remained laughing belowdecks.

Gaining Respect

Another time, he was sitting at a table, down below, having a pleasant after-work drink with his shipmates, when he suddenly blew out the candles and pulled out his two huge pistols. Before anyone could get a word out, he shot right under the table, smashing the knee of Israel Hands, his second in command, who was taken immediately to the wooden leg department.

When the others rather falteringly asked why exactly he'd done it, Blackbeard replied quite calmly that if he didn't shoot one of his crew every now and again, they might forget exactly who he was—which is fair enough, I suppose.

Caution

Further research suggests that some of these stories are exaggeratons—made up by the great novelist and historian (and fibber) Daniel Defoe (who'd say anything to sell a few more books). True, Edward Teach, alias Blackbeard, was very much on the wrong side of respectability. And true you wouldn't want him to marry your sister, but there is no documented record of his ever really killing or torturing anyone for a laugh.

But, nonetheless, he did commit some gross acts of piracy, did cheat his crew out of most of their share of the bounty, and did manage to die in the most spectacular manner.

Blackbeard Backs Out—Ungracefully

On November 17, 1718, two naval sloops sailed south to capture Edward Teach who by now had a hefty price (and his famous wide-brimmed hat) on his head. They caught up with him five days later at the Ocracoke Inlet, North Carolina— the old blackguard's favorite hideout. When Blackbeard realized who they were, he laughed heartily, downed a huge tankard of rum, and yelled across to the officers on the other boat: "Damnation to anyone who should give or ask quarter [mercy]." Which was pretty rude, you must admit.

Young Lieutenant Robert Maynard, who was in command of one of the naval sloops, shouted back, "I shall expect no quarter from you and shall give none." Fighting talk in anyone's language.

The Pick of the Bunch

After an all-out fight between the ships, the two captains finally came face to horrible face on Maynard's deck, which Blackbeard and his merry men had boarded without so much as an invitation. First they fought with pistols. Blackbeard's missed due to his inebriated state, but Maynard's hit home, unfortunately having absolutely no effect whatsoever. Then, just like in the movies, it was cutlasses. They fought hard until poor Maynard's blade was broken in two. Then, just as Maynard stepped back to cock his other pistol, Blackbeard lumbered forward for the kill. Unfortunately (for Blackbeard), a naval seaman jumped in his way and slashed him right across the throat as he passed, causing him to spout a frothy fountain of blood and generally make a terrible mess everywhere. The brave lieutenant, now ready, managed to shoot Blackbeard again but, once more, it didn't stop him. But another slash from a broadsword right across the back of his neck did. (I'm surprised his head didn't fall right off.) Well, it did stop him, but it still didn't bring him down. The old sea dog, bleeding and cursing, wavered for what seemed a long time trying desperately to cock another of his many pistols. Eventually, however, he crashed, like a bewildered bull in a bullring, to the blood-soaked deck—stone cold dead. When they finally examined his body, they found twenty-five separate wounds. All the other pirates, by the way, either surrendered or dived over the sides before you could say "shiver my timbers."

They hadn't even waited to see the boss's huge head finally being severed from his huge body and stuck triumphantly on the front of Maynard's sloop as a grisly trophy.

Bartholomew Roberts—The Cleverest

Welshman Bartholemew Roberts, born in 1682, had been an honest, hardworking seaman both in the Royal Navy and on merchant ships for more than thirty years. He was a natural sailor but realized, like Blackbeard, that his dream of becoming a captain was never going to happen—certainly not on the right side of the law.

His life of villainy started almost by accident. He was second mate on a slave ship called the *Princess* when it (and he) were captured by another Welshman, pirate captain Howell Davis in his ship the *Rover*. Davis actually liked Roberts but couldn't persuade him to join in the pirate fun. It was only when Davis was shot dead during a daring raid that the swarthy crew asked Bartholomew if he'd like to be their captain (they hadn't any idea how to sail the silly boat). Forget this thing about being a prisoner for an adventure, Roberts thought, and decided to reject king and country and accept the generous offer. Let's face it, if you're going to be a pirate, you might as well be the captain!

Bartholomew Roberts or Black Bart (as he was soon nicknamed) was to become probably the greatest pirate captain ever. There was no more spectacular mariner to be found in all the seven seas, and no one was more flamboyant. In his red vest and breeches, a red feather stuck in his tricorn, wearing a flashy diamond cross on a thick gold chain and two pairs of pistols hanging off a red silk sling over his shoulders, he was a brilliant sight.

On his first trip, he struck gold—literally—running into a fleet of forty-two Portuguese ships parked in the harbor of Bahia (now Salvador) on the Brazilian coast, waiting for an armed escort. The first boat they attacked turned out to be the richest, and Black Bart and his crew escaped with a haul of 90,000 gold moidores and chests of fabulous jewelry. The

BARTHOLOMEW ROBERTS

latter included that priceless diamond cross specially made for the king of Portugal, which the pirate captain was to wear at all times. Almost best of all the loot were the bales of fine tobacco. Not a shot had been fired.

Black Bart was an extraordinary fellow, being very cruel on the one hand but terribly fair on the other. His code of rules on board ship was designed so that each man should be treated equally and honestly—odd on a ship whose sole purpose was to rob and kill with maximum barbarity.

Bart's Rules (well, some of them):

- All candles were to be out by eight o'clock—bedtime. Anyone who wanted to carry on drinking had to do it on deck—and quietly.

- No fighting allowed on board. All arguments were to be settled on land under the supervision of the quartermaster. The rivals were first asked to fight a duel with pistols. If they both missed, they switched to swords. The winner was the first to draw blood.
- No gambling or women were allowed on board. Women prisoners were protected by armed guards.

On one occasion, when mildly insulted by a drunken crew member, Roberts ran the poor guy through with his sword on the spot. Someone else in the crew, a fellow called Jones, yet another Welshman, thought this unfair and had the nerve to curse the captain and attack him, throwing him clean over a cannon. A mini-mutiny looked imminent, but, at the quartermaster's quickly convened inquiry, it was decided for the whole business to work (being pirates and all), that the captain must be respected and obeyed at all times and that Jones should have two lashes of the cat-o'-nine-tails from

each member of the crew. This normally wouldn't have been so bad, but at that time there were 180 of 'em.

On another occasion in 1722, when one of eleven British slave ships failed to surrender, Roberts's crew poured tar over the deck and set fire to the ship with eighty slaves on board, still chained together in pairs. This created a huge problem for the victims. They could either leap over the side and be lunch (double portion) for the sharks that were waiting in the surrounding waters or stay to be roasted alive. What a choice!

Black Bart and his crew of sixty were to become legendary throughout the Caribbean and around the African coast for their sheer nerve and stupendous sailing ability, at times attacking up to twenty-six ships at a time.

Vendetta

Roberts had a fixation about sailors from either of the islands of Martinique or Barbados because of their governors' constant and annoying attempts to catch him. If he ever captured any pirates from these two island nations, he would either cat-o'-nine-tail them almost to a pulp, cut off their ears, or tie them to the mainmast and use them for target practice. (Not their ears—the sailors!) Once, when capturing a ship sailing out of Martinique, Roberts discovered to his great glee that the ship was carrying the island's governor. Black Bart thought it a great joke to have him hanged from the yardarm and left dangling there for the rest of the trip.

Roberts died as he had lived, attacking a far stronger naval vessel, the *Swallow*, that had been trying for eight months to catch him. The brave buccaneer, not yet forty, had his throat ripped open by some stray grapeshot. His crew were instantly broken and disillusioned without him (some even cried out loud—big sissies) and were soon captured. Actually it was later revealed that most of them were still drunk from the merriment of the night before and couldn't have fought to save their miserable lives. Many of those captured, unfortunately (depending on which way you look at it), died on their way to trial, but it would hardly have done them any good if they hadn't, for, all in all, fifty-two were hanged and eighteen of the very worst were cut down, tarred, and hung in cages from gibbets till they eventually rotted right down to their bare bones.

Edward (Ned) Low—The Cruelest

Another brilliant mariner, Edward Low, was a Londoner, born at the beginning of the eighteenth century. As a boy, he couldn't read or write and made a living by stealing coins off other boys and beating them up if they objected. As a youngster, he immigrated to Boston, Massachusetts, and began work as a ship rigger (the only honest thing he ever did) before going to sea in 1721. Low soon disagreed with his first captain and even fired a shot at him. Luckily it missed, but unluckily it blew the brains out of another crew member who was carelessly standing behind him.

WHOOPS— SORRY!

Low stole the small boat that the crew used to go to shore and, with a few shipmates, took off, captured a ship, and headed for Jamaica, where they ran up a black flag and decided to try piracy. It became his chosen calling, and before long he was plundering numerous ships and having success throughout the Caribbean. But all this was kids' stuff, and Low eventually captured a magnificent schooner that he took a fancy to and appropriately called her the *Fancy*. He then hired more men and went pirating in earnest.

His reputation grew within a year, not only for the boats he robbed, but for the enormous cruelty he used while doing it. The stories of his barbarity are legendary, especially against the Spaniards and the French, whom he hated. At one time, he overtook a Spanish privateer and on examination discovered it had taken prisoner a group of captains from recently overhauled American ships. Low wasn't wild about Americans at the best of times, but at least they weren't Spaniards. On the basis of the old pirate saying—"dead men tell no tales"—he promptly slaughtered everyone aboard. Any that went over the side in terror were relentlessly pursued in boats and clubbed senseless as they tried to swim for safety. He then burned the ship and sank her.

Admiral Low (as he eventually called himself) wasn't an admirer of the Portuguese either. He once took a Portuguese ship on its way home from Brazil with a fortune in gold on board. Well, not actually on board. The captain had hung the coins in a large sack outside his cabin window. When he saw the pirate ship bearing down on him, he cut the sack loose and let it sink to the bottom of the ocean (where it presumably still is). For this Mr. Low cut off the captain's lips, boiled them in oil, and then murdered his thirty-two shipmates in front of him. That must really redefine "angry."

At the end of his career, when he was on the run from HMS *Greyhound*, he became so furious at the ship's persistence that he decided to take it out on anyone he came across. First to come along was a large whaling sloop. For no good reason, he stripped the poor captain naked and cut off his ears before shooting him through the head (at least he couldn't hear the bang!). Then, again for no reason, he sent the poor crew off in a little whaling boat with nothing more than a couple of dry biscuits, some water, and a compass. But worse was still to come. A day or so later, he took the captains of two more whaling boats on board his ship. He disemboweled one of them, then took out his heart, cooked it, and forced one of his crew to eat it. The other one was

slashed mercilessly, before being made to eat his own ears, which had been roasted but luckily sprinkled with salt and pepper (unfortunately ketchup hadn't been invented). There's no record of the poor unfortunate not enjoying the meal, but they do say he died later of his injuries.

Eventually, Low was set upon by his crew for murdering the quartermaster in his sleep after an argument, and was put overboard with a couple of his shipmates in a little boat with no provisions. They were in luck—well, sort of. They were picked up by a ship shortly afterward. But it was a French ship (the French were after Low and company even more than anyone else). The French crew threw him and his shipmates in irons and took them off to Martinique, where they were tried and then hanged for crimes against humanity. Or were they? Some historians tell another story—that Low escaped and disappeared off the face of the earth.

Henry Morgan—The Most Successful

Yet *another* Welshman (I give up), Henry Morgan, was born in 1635 into a well-to-do military family. Henry wanted to be a soldier and joined the expeditionary force of 7,000 troops sent to capture the Spanish stronghold of Hispaniola. When that didn't work, he decided to attack Jamaica, which turned out to be an easy target.

Gradually Morgan got to lead his own raids on

CAPTAIN MORGAN

Jamaica, and he gained great fame as one of the most fierce and feared enemies of the Spaniards. When Edward Mansfield, the leader of the privateers (respectable pirates), was executed by the Spaniards, Morgan was chosen to replace him. Thus, at only thirty-two, he became admiral of the Brethren of the Coast, a wily band of buccaneers and ill-disguised cutthroat pirates. Their greatest coup was to capture the Spanish stronghold and largest port in South America, Portobelo, against ridiculous odds. He then sent a snide letter to the Spanish governor saying he could have his town back for a ton of money or Morgan would burn the place to the ground. After much toing and froing, Morgan walked (or sailed) away with a hefty treasure in gold coins, silver bars, and chests chock-full of silver plate. Everyone back home in Britain was overjoyed, and Morgan was an overnight superhero. But by now Henry had got the taste for money and was soon out aplundering once more.

Got a Light?

After one such raid, Morgan and his boys celebrated so hard and became so drunk that someone accidentally dropped a lighted something or other near the gunpowder supply, and the whole ship was blown to smithereens. Our Henry, lucky as ever, was picked up in the sea, a trifle damp but otherwise okay—one of only ten survivors.

Captain Henry Morgan went on to wreak more havoc among the Spaniards, but as he did so he gained a reputation for cruelty far beyond what was necessary. His destruction of Panama City went down in history as an orgy of looting, killing, and torture that has seldom been equaled. More to the point, many of his attacks occurred after a peace treaty had already been signed between Britain and Spain, a fact that naturally got him into deep trouble. Also, he was terribly unfair when it came to sharing the spoils with his crew, always taking the lion's share for himself.

Despite all this, the admittedly brave captain still led a charmed life and was knighted in 1674 and sent back to Jamaica as its lieutenant governor. The ultimate joke was that in the following years, until his death in 1668, the fabulously wealthy Sir Henry Morgan spent most of his time suppressing buccaneering and piracy, hanging hundreds of his former colleagues and associates. All this was ironic—not to mention two-faced—when you come to think of it.

God Speaks?

In 1692 Port Royal, reputedly the most wicked town in the Western Hemisphere, was destroyed by a massive earthquake, burying forever the tomb of the notorious and illustrious Henry Morgan.

Stede Bonnet—The Most Cultured

Major Stede Bonnet was different from all the other pirates and buccaneers. Born in 1688, he became a respected, educated, and extremely cultured man of letters and went into piracy merely to get away from his missus whose nagging was driving him around the bend (or out to sea). Bonnet had owned a substantial sugar plantation on the island of Barbados until, suddenly, without warning and knowing about as much as you or I do about the sea, disappeared. Secretly, he'd fitted out a fast sloop, which he called the *Revenge*, with ten guns and an extensive library of his favorite books, had assembled a crew of seventy similarly minded men and then simply sailed off into the sunset to look for fame and fortune—brilliant stuff! And wasn't he good at it. After lots of fun on the high seas, he eventually ended up in the same raiding group as Blackbeard. Along with the *Revenge* (now sporting thirty guns and a crew of 300), he became, like Edward Teach, a big name in the world of piracy. The debonair major, by the way, took no part in the actual sailing but strolled the deck in a silk morning gown, drink in one hand and one of his many volumes in the other.

Later on, a contrite Bonnet managed to sweet-talk his way into a pardon for his dastardly deeds and was even given a privateer's commission to act against the Spaniards (he could now rob, murder, and pillage legally). But the miffed major had a few old scores to settle with Blackbeard, who'd cheated him out of a large share of loot. So, instead of going after the Spaniards, like he'd promised, he set out in the opposite direction to chase the old dog down. He soon forgot all about privateering. Changing his name to Captain Roberts and his sloop's to the *Royal James*, he started robbing and looting with new passion.

Bonnet (alias Roberts) was eventually captured after a long, bloodthirsty, and spectacular chase, and he and his men were brought to Charleston for trial. At the trial, the judge really let Bonnet have it for committing eleven acts of piracy after he'd been pardoned for killing eighteen naval men who'd been sent to get him. Bonnet was apparently shocked at the death sentence and was taken groveling, posy in hand, and making an awful fuss, to be hanged with the rest of his men at a special gallows in Charleston Harbor.

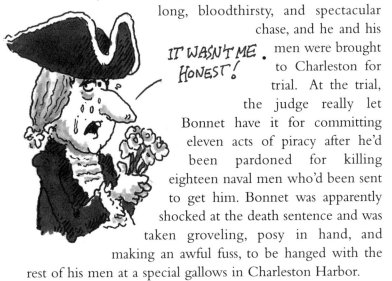

IT WASN'T ME. HONEST!

François L'Olonnois—The All-around Nastiest

There's bad pirates, there's very bad pirates, and then, way out in front in the badness stakes there's François L'Olonnois. Born Jean David Nau, at the back end of the seventeenth century, he started life as a lowly bonded servant on one of the West Indian islands before moving to the pirate island of Hispaniola. He then became one of the early boucaniers. Then he joined with others to start real buccaneering, first from canoes and then from small ships that they captured. The young Frenchman was noted for his almost lunatic courage and was soon given a commission to try to take the big Spanish treasure ships.

After many hair-raising adventures, he was eventually reported dead to the governor of Cuba. But the wily old governor didn't believe it and sent a posse of ships to track him down. They eventually did.

But it all ended up with L'Olonnois, on board the ship that had been attacking him, personally chopping off the heads, one by one, of all those who'd hidden below decks, as they poked their heads out to see what was going on. All except one, who was spared simply so he could report back to the governor.

The vicious pirate's small armada gradually grew to eight separate ships with 700 men, and together they robbed and plundered and murdered as far as Mexico and Nicaragua. They looted small coastal cities to the tune of 260,000 pieces of eight. The stories of their cruel and unrelenting torture almost defy belief.

As an example, when a prisoner claimed he didn't know the route to his hometown, which L'Olonnois was trying to reach and plunder, the monster ripped him open, tore out his heart, chewed on it, and then threw it in the face of his friend saying that he'd do the same to him if he didn't play ball.

Eventually, by poetic justice, L'Olonnois himself was captured by a band of grumpy Indians, who took great delight in hacking him limb from limb, cooking him in a big pot, and then eating him for supper.

MMM! I LOVE FRENCH FOOD

HANGING AROUND

If piracy had become your chosen profession, it was generally regarded as a bad idea to get caught. Then as now, any kind of illegal behavior on the high seas was likely to make the powers-that-be (or were) very annoyed. In the pirates' and mutineers' cases, the trial was generally an open and shut one—no warnings, reprimands, or light fines, etc. The penalty—death by public hanging—was almost inevitable. London was a favorite place for hanging, particularly in the neighborhood of Wapping—a murky, smelly, labyrinth of docks, gin shops, wharves, alehouses, brothels, and boat builders, all crammed together in a tangle of rope-strewn masts.

Between Wapping New Stairs and King Henry's Stairs, as they are called today, was the notorious Execution Dock, a gallows designed purely for punishing pirates. These unfortunates were destined to "dance the hempen jig" on a rope just above the waterline at low tide. There they would be hanged pathetically just above the oozing mud, as the filthy Thames River covered their limp bodies for three tides—a symbol of the jurisdiction of Britain's Lord High Admiral. He was the guy whose job it was to oversee the punishment of all those who did their dirty deeds on the high seas and waterways up to low tide mark. Crimes committed above the tide mark were tried by the civil courts. On the other side of the river, built on piles, stood the ancient Angel Inn, where that old tyrant Judge George Jeffreys (the hanging judge) would sit having a quiet drink while watching his condemned subjects being "turned off," as he so charmingly put it, across the water (beats darts, I suppose).

Up until 1723, only the captain and the quartermaster of a pirate ship would have actually been hanged, but the war against piracy became so frenzied that it was decided to string up anyone who'd even sniffed a pirate boat, let alone sailed under the Jolly Roger. Except, of course, for those who'd been captured at sea and forced into it. Needless to say, the most common defense of your average accused pirate was that he had been made to sign the pirates' articles (and who can blame him), but they seldom got away with their crimes because they were usually incriminated by the ones who'd already been told they were going to swing. Others swore blind that they knew the whereabouts of lots of other pirates and would help track them down if their lives were spared. There really is no honor among thieves or pirates.

THICK AS A PIRATE ↓

Execution Day

An execution was a fun day out for the average London family in the sixteenth and seventeenth centuries. And the demise of a dastardly pirate was probably the best gig of all. Hours before it happened, crowds would arrive at Execution Dock from both sides of the river—at that time it was relatively easy to cross by horse and cart at low tide. Not only that, but boats would sail upriver and downriver (at high tide) to moor near the gallows to get the best view possible. Such a laugh!

Eventually the dismal procession would arrive from either the Newgate or Marshalsea Prisons, led by the Admiral Marshal carrying a silver oar (to prove his authority). The pirate or pirates in question would be manacled in a heavily guarded cart, and they would sometimes chink their chains cheekily to the throng of leering Londoners who would hurl the most obscene abuse (and worse!) as they passed. It was a tradition for pirates to die with as much bravado as possible, so they would often dress in their finest clothes, festooned in red and blue ribbons. One even kicked his footwear into the crowd, joking that he could never be seen to die with his shoes on.

The gibbet at Execution Dock was a relatively simple affair—just two vertical posts and a cross member from which the rope or ropes would dangle. The pirate would be asked (not very nicely) to climb up a shortish ladder, where a noose would be put over his head. All the executioner had to do was pull the ladder away. Money for old rope! In those days hanging did not always kill the customer immediately, especially if their neck didn't break at the first drop, so it was quite common for relatives to swing on their nearest and dearest's legs to hasten his horrible end—a grisly sight, but just what the audience ordered. After the three tides had washed over them, the buccaneers' bodies would either be thrown into unmarked graves or hung up again in special cages. These were positioned along various parts of the river, until the bodies rotted to their bare bones—a warning to any other ordinary sailors who thought they might like a bit of light piracy.

NOW YOU KNOW HOW I FEEL

The Kidd Gets It

In 1701 the body of the notorious villain Captain William Kidd, who'd been kept for a year in the hideous Newgate Prison, was hung on a special gibbet at Tilbury Point. He was put in a terrifying harness of iron hoops and chains, so that mariners could observe his rotting, crow-pecked corpse for more than an hour as they swept around that wide and desolate part of the Thames. Even more eerie, he'd been 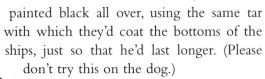 painted black all over, using the same tar with which they'd coat the bottoms of the ships, just so that he'd last longer. (Please don't try this on the dog.)

The cage was constructed of strong iron, firstly so that relatives couldn't steal the body to give it a decent burial and secondly so that the skeleton could be held in place once the flesh had rotted or been pecked away by the crows.

Across the Atlantic and around the Caribbean, it was a similar deal. Convicted pirates would dangle on special gibbets planted on the little outcrops. These poked above the water at the approaches to those Caribbean islands the pirates had terrorized for so long. On the East Coast, around Charleston, South Carolina, or Newport, Rhode Island, and particularly Boston, justice was short and swift, with pirates hung out like bunting at a fairground.

Sometimes, if the pirates knew that there was no escaping the rope, they went out fighting in great style. On one occasion in 1720, a pirate awaiting his death in the colony of Virginia demanded a bottle of wine and, as he swigged a glass, "Drank Damnation to the Governor and Confusion to the Colony."

In Britain between 1716 and 1726, over 400 convicted pirates were executed. The rest went to a fate that some thought even worse—they were imprisoned on dreaded hulks. These were decommissioned sloops and galleons that were moored in the vast lonely estuary of the Thames and used as prisons.

French Treat

Captured French corsairs (commissioned pirates) were often sent to these miserable Thames hulks where they were treated even worse. In 1797 one such prisoner was recorded as saying, "For the last eight weeks we have been reduced to eating dogs, cats, and rats . . . the only rations we get consist of moldy bread . . . rotten meat, and brackish water." That's rich, I reckon, coming from a country that gobbles up snails and the back legs off frogs at the drop of a chapeau, but we won't go into that now!

Forgotten

The Spanish pirate Antonio Mendoza had it even worse. The authorities of Saint Christopher in the West Indies cut off his ears, burned out his tongue with a red-hot iron, and left him literally to rot in a forgotten dungeon.

From around the middle of the eighteenth century, the general public didn't at all view pirates as heroes. Anyone who had to travel on the high seas would have been at their mercy. Pirates were generally regarded as enemies of all humankind, and it must be said that the relentless and savage hangings certainly acted as a deterrent to anyone contemplating answering a pirate help-wanted ad.

Timescale

Although the golden age for pirates was only really between the mid-seventeenth and the early eighteenth centuries, the very first hanging for robbery on the high seas was in 1228 and the very last as recently as 1840.

The End of the Voyage

The Golden Age of Piracy came to a speedy finale in the early nineteenth century when a massive $500,000 was set aside to create a special crack American squadron under Commodore David Porter. He put together eight superfast schooners, a newfangled steam-powered warship, and five flat-bottomed landing craft to attack the buccaneers when ashore. Last and most brilliant of all, he added the ultimate sitting duck—a ship that looked just like a ponderous old merchant vessel but that was packed with six massive cannons. With a gang of 1,500 tough marines, this little armada joined the six hard-worked U.S. warships that were already in the Caribbean searching for the bewildered buccaneers. In a couple of years, the game was up, hundreds of pirates were captured or killed, and the rest simply disappeared into thin air.

One of the very last acts of piracy in the Atlantic Ocean took place on September 20, 1832, when the pirate ship *Panda* intercepted an American brig, the *Mexican*. The U.S. ship just happened to be carrying $20,000 worth of silver bars to Argentina from the East Coast. When the pirates politely asked their captain, a mean-spirited fellow called Pedro Gilbert, what to do with the captives, he replied rather oddly, "dead cats don't mew, you know what to do"—obviously a feline version of the old pirate saying "dead men tell no tales." The pirate crew promptly relieved the ship of its silver, ordered the crew downstairs, chucked in a load of oil-soaked rags, battened down the hatches, and set fire to what they planned would become the poor innocents' floating coffin. The crew luckily broke out but cleverly kept the fire going until the pirate ship was over the horizon (just in case they came back). A few months later, Gilbert and company were caught loading slaves on the African coast by a British warship, which took them immediately to Boston and hanged 'em.

But that was then, and this is now. Piracy, I have to report, is back, and with a vengeance. Not as it was in the past—ragged brigands in romantic sailing ships, armed with cutlasses, muskets, and cannons and stuff—but highly professional criminals in high-speed cruisers, armed to the teeth with rocket launchers, careering around the Indian Ocean and the South China Sea, hijacking cargo boats and private yachts for all they're worth. There's not a parrot or a wooden leg in sight. Likewise, the prizes are also different—no Spanish gold or Aztec jewelry these days. According to international security agencies, modern pirates go after stuff they can move and sell easily: boring stuff like paint, rope, and household commodities. But the modern pirates are just as ruthless, often tying up the crew and leaving them on board their ship while it ploughs ahead through busy, congested waters. As a defense against this new surge in maritime crime, the International Maritime Bureau's Piracy Reporting Centre was set up in 1992 in Malaysia where owners and captains alike can telephone to report anything suspicious.

But it's kind of like trying to turn back the very sea they sail in. Wherever there is a defenseless vessel bobbing around on a big, lonely ocean, there will always be those who think it might be fun to teach them a lesson they'll never forget. I don't know about you, but I think that if we'd never had pirates, I, for one, would miss 'em.

PIRATE SPEAK

the Admiralty: the group of stuffy old officers who once had general authority over British naval affairs. This also refers to the courts and the system of laws that ruled the seas.

Barbary Coast: the northern coast of Africa, extending from Egypt to the Atlantic Ocean. The Barbary pirates wreaked havoc on Mediterranean shipping for 300 years.

buccaneer: a plundering, loot-taking person operating outside the law (no commission in sight!) in the West Indies

bully beef: the delicious (not!) pickled beef carried in barrels on board ship

Caribbean islands: various islands, such as Barbados, Jamaica, and Hispaniola, that lie in the Caribbean Sea and were among the main haunts of some of the world's worst pirates

commission: formal authorization to perform specific acts. In pirate speak, a commission gave the bearer the right to attack the ships belonging to the enemies of one's country.

corsair: a plundering, loot-taking person operating outside the law along the Barbary Coast

cutlass: a short, curved sword used by sailors and pirates

gibbet: an upright post with a projecting arm that was used to hang the bodies of executed criminals

heave-ho!: a phrase used by sailors and pirates pulling hard on a rope

Lord High Admiral: the top official in the British Admiralty (not a person to mess with!)

merchant ship: a privately owned vessel that carries cargo to sell or trade—the favorite prey of pirates, buccaneers, corsairs, and bad guys of all kinds

oakum: rope smothered in tar used to fill in gaps between a ship's planks (and horrid work it was)

parts of a ship: deck (the flat top); hold (the cargo area beneath the deck); hull (the curved bottom); mainmast (the tallest and most important spar, or pole)

press-gang: a group of oh-so-friendly men who are empowered to force other men into naval or pirate service

privateer: an armed private sailor licensed to attack enemy shipping. Broadly, privateers attacked pretty much anything they liked, more or less without fear of being chased by the law.

quartermaster: the officer in charge of the helm and navigation equipment (one of your more important ship colleagues)

Royal Navy: in Britain, the arm of the service devoted to maritime activities, including shipbuilding, operating naval stations, and training naval personnel. A lot of our favorite pirates started out in the Royal Navy, where they learned their trade but got very little pay.

schooner: a two-masted vessel, with a foremast and a mainmast that are placed nearly amidships

trade route: a sea-lane used by merchant ships. Usually, a trade route had known—though not always reliable—weather patterns

West Indies: a large group of Caribbean islands between North and South America

FURTHER READING

Black, Clinton V. *Pirates of the West Indies.* New York: Cambridge University Press, 1989.

Hague, Michael. *The Book of Pirates.* New York: HarperCollins Publishers, 2001.

Hawes, Charles Boardman. *The Dark Frigate.* New York: Little, Brown & Company, 1996.

Kallen, Stuart A. *Life Among the Pirates.* San Diego, CA: Lucent Books, 1999.

Lawrence, Iain. *The Buccaneers.* New York: Delacorte, 2001.

———. *The Smugglers.* New York: Delacorte, 1999.

———. *The Wreckers.* New York: Delacorte, 1998.

Lindgren, Astrid. *The Adventures of Pippi Longstocking.* New York: Viking Children's Books, 1997.

Meltzer, Milton. *Piracy and Plunder: A Murderous Business.* New York: Dutton Books, 2001.

Platt, Richard. *Eyewitness: Pirate.* New York: DK Publishing, 2000.

Sharp, Anne W. *Daring Women Pirates.* Minneapolis, MN: Lerner Publications Company, 2002.

Stevenson, Robert Louis. *Treasure Island.* New York: Atheneum, 1981.

Walker, Richard. *The Barefoot Book of Pirates.* Cambridge, MA: Barefoot Books, 1998.

Weatherly, Myra. *Women Pirates: Eight Stories of Adventure.* Greensboro, NC: Morgan Reynolds, 1998.

WEBSITES

General Information

Pyrate's Providence
  <http://www.inkyfingers.com/pyrates>
CyberInk Pirates!
  <http://www.yohoyoho.com>
The Pirate's Library
  <http://www.ferncanyonpress.com/pirates.html>
Pirates, Privateers, Swashbucklers, and Fops
  <http://www.legends.dm.net/index.html>

Pirates in Paradise

History of the Bahamas
  <http://www.geographia.com/bahamas>
Nassau Tourism
  <http://www.pirates-of-nassau.com>

Pirate Shipwrecks Discovered

Pirate Ghosts
  <http://www.discovery.com/stories/history/pirates/pirates.html>
Pirates of the Whydah
  <http://www.nationalgeographic.com/whydah/main.html>
Blackbeard's Queen Anne's Revenge
  <http://www.blackbeard.eastnet.ecu.edu/main.html>
Tales from the Deep
  <http://www.whyfiles.org/036pirates>
North Carolina Maritime Museum
  <http://www.ah.dcr.state.nc.us/qar>

INDEX

ABOUT THE AUTHOR

John Farman has worked as a commercial illustrator and a cartoonist and has written more than thirty nonfiction books for children. He lives in London, England.